Place, Church and Mission

Stephen Radley

Priest-in-Charge, Marley Hill

Education and Training Officer
for the Deaneries of Gateshead and Gateshead West

GROVE BOOKS LIMITED
RIDLEY HALL RD CAMBRIDGE CB3 9HU

Contents

1. Introduction 3
2. What is Place? 6
3. Place and Relationships 13
4. Place and Church 17

Acknowledgments

This booklet would not have been written without the influence of three people. Much of the theoretical content emerged during the preparation of a thesis for an MA at Durham University. The patient, tolerant guidance of my supervisor, Dan Hardy, was important then and the continuing influence will be obvious. My interest in place, born in a geography degree, was encouraged by an observation made, by chance, by Michael Vasey. His continuing friendship and the stimulation provided by conversations and the criticisms of some Cranmer Hall students to these ideas have helped me keep up with some more recent writing while working full-time in parish ministry. The love and encouragement of my wife Jane is beyond words and without it there would not have been the belief that it was worth pursuing the ideas.

The Cover Illustration is by Peter Ashton

Copyright © Stephen Radley 1997

First Impression June 1997
ISSN 0144-171X
ISBN 1 85174 345 6

1
Introduction

> 'The days of man are but as grass:
> he flourishes like a flower of the field;
> when the wind goes over it, it is gone:
> and its place will know it no more.'
> Psalm 103.15,16

In these verses from Psalm 103 the Psalmist portrays 'place' as an active, knowing subject. In the *ASB* funeral service, which draws on Psalm 103, 'Man' is likened to a flower and he is passive and known by the place of which he is a part. This booklet explores how human beings operate in place and investigates the biblical observation about the human condition with respect to place—a human being is a knowing subject constrained by an inanimate agent.

Genesis and Exodus are concerned, amongst other things, with journey. Abraham and Moses have no place of their own; they do not belong. Brueggemann describes Moses as a 'sojourner' or 'resident alien' and then a wanderer. Like Jesus' temptation wilderness, the wilderness in which the Israelites wandered was not a period of refreshing retreat. Although on the way to the fulfilment of promise, the wilderness is a place of unrest, of defeat, of the way being lost, punctuated by moments of revelation.[1]

The Promised Land, a defining category of Israel's chosenness and nationhood, is an expression of God's love for his people. But in the New Testament, and since, the journey to a 'spiritualized' Promised Land (heaven) becomes the lens through which physical places are viewed. Just as Christ is our peace (Eph 2.14a), so by implication he is our place. Our relationship with God is no longer through a particular place, in a particular building (the Temple), but through Jesus.

But the spiritualizing of the physical is not enough. It responds appropriately to the theological issue of the Promised Land but obscures an account of being in place. It does not express an interest in the universal experience of living in a place, of being placed in a social environment or of feelings of belonging, or not belonging, to a place. There is no theological anthropology and little attempt to give a theological account of what it is to live a human

---

[1] W Brueggeman makes these observation in *The Land* (Philadelphia: Fortress Press, 1977) pp 6-9.

life here and now.[2] And, consequently, there is no possibility of organizing the church or planning our mission around the realities of present human experience. Human lives are lived in the material, sense world, a world which is touched, heard and seen, a world which is created. It mattered to Moses that he would never live where he belonged not just because the Promised Land was a spiritual home but because it was also a physical home. The promise of the Land to the Israelites tells us most about the love of God for his people, his desire that they should be 'a light to the nations' and about his faithful fulfilment of his promise to Abraham—but it also shows important universal truths about being human.

Living in a place, making sense of that place and being placed in human society are universal experiences which form the backdrop to the history of the Israelites in the Promised Land. And in the process it anchors the church's self-understanding as belonging to another place in the experience of living in this place. To be aware of our spiritual home in Christ only reinforces our awareness of our living in a created world as social beings. Our experiences of place are meant to be, even if they are imperfect.

Much of the modern world denies the importance of the place.[3] We live private, individual lives, drive to supermarkets which are inaccessible on foot and which show little or no regional character. We even commute to church, or at least many of us do. We are encouraged to move from one part of the country to another in the search for work. Some rural communities retain a fierce sense of independence, especially in ecclesial matters, and mobility in former pit villages here in the North East is low. But these examples are rare and peripheral to most of British society which is based on individual households and the combustion engine.

The question of how place operates is of great importance to modern society, for our assumptions about the neutrality and passivity of place are mistaken. It is also of great importance for the church because we have inadvertently adopted a number of competing contemporary attitudes to place. These cloud our consideration of issues such as the value of the parish, the role of eclectic churches and other non-geographical modes of being church, sector ministry, and the location of mission. The church is aware of the presence of questions about place but unsure how to respond. Dominant pictures of the church such as the Body of Christ or the People of God are used in ways which do not make any reference to the place in which the people or

---

2   An alternative account of the material world which does not deny its importance is found in Celtic thought about place. The natural landscape is an icon. or boundary place 'between the material world and the other world.' See P Sheldrake. *Living Between Worlds* (London: DLT. 1995) p 7.
3   There has been a long tradition in Western thought in which the language of ideas. of spirituality and of the soul is preferred to the language of the material. of creation and of embodiment.

INTRODUCTION

the body finds itself. By contrast, in the New Testament, the church is a people, or body of Christ, in a place.[4] Modern patterns of behaviour have complicated the meaning of locality and an important debate exists about what 'local' means in a mobile, individualized culture. This booklet offers a description of how place works, an understanding of place from a trinitarian perspective and some observations and suggestions about place and the church: an understanding of locality, a flexible working of the Anglican parish system and the collaborative ministry of church leaders, lay and ordained.

---

4   I am grateful to Michael Vasey for this observation—see, for example, 1 Cor 1.2.

2
What is Place?

Describing the complex emotions and feelings a place can evoke Penelope Lively writes of a man walking in central London and reading the place names on the front of buses:

> 'A column of buses stand pulsing in a traffic jam: Gospel Oak, Putney Heath, Clapton Pond, Wood Green. Matthew and Alice pause on the pavement and he thinks of the city flung out all around, invisible and inviolate. He forgets, for an instant, his own concerns, and feels the power of the place, its resonances, its charge of life, its coded narrative. He reads the buses and sees that the words are the silt of all that has been here— hills and rivers, woods and fields, trade, worship, customs and events, and the unquenchable evidence of language. The city mutters still in Anglo-Saxon; it remembers the hills that have become Neasden and Islington and Hendon, the marshy islands of Battersea and Bermondsey. The ghost of another topography lingers; the uplands and the streams, the wood and fords are inscribed still on the London Streetfinder, on the ubiquitous geometry of the underground map, in the destination of buses. The Fleet River, its last physical trickle locked away underground in a cast iron pipe, leaves its name defiant and untamed upon the surface. The whole place is one babble of allusion, all chronology subsumed into distortions and mutations of today, so that in the end what is visible and what is uttered are complementary. The jumbled brick and stone of the city's landscape is a medley of style in which centuries and decades rub shoulders in a disorder that denies the sequence of time. Language takes up the theme, and religion, battles and conquests, kings and queens and potentates, that reach back a thousand years or ten, providing in the end a dictionary of reference for those who will listen. Cheapside, Temple, Trafalgar, Quebec, a profligacy of Victorias and Georges and Cumberlands and Bedfords—there is all, on a million pairs of lips every day, on and on, the imperishable clamour of those who have been before.'[5]

Lively illustrates, inadvertently, the three ways in which human beings function in place and, additionally, the ways in which place impinges on human beings. In this first section we will describe these three ways.

---

5 P Lively, *City of the Mind* (London: Penguin, 1992) pp 66-67.

WHAT IS PLACE?

Feeling 'At Home': Existential Place

The 'jumbled brick and stone of the city's landscape' means something to Matthew as his mind is diverted from his own concerns by the 'babble of allusion' which is the place. When he reads 'Gospel Oak' or 'Bermondsey' on the front of a bus there are pictures which come into his mind of those places. He will have an experience of the place by feeling 'at home' or not feeling 'at home' in the place. In the mid 1970s Eduard Relph, a Canadian geographer, wrote about feelings of belonging and not belonging in the place where one lives.[6] He wrote that:

'To be human is to live in a world that is filled with significant places: to be human is to have and to know *your* place.'[7]

His account of human attachment to particular places develops the twin concepts of 'outsideness' and 'insideness.' He defines insideness by saying that:

'To be inside a place is to belong to it and to identify with it, and the more profoundly inside you are the stronger is this identity with the place.'[8]

Insideness is a feeling of identification with a place but it can take several forms and Relph identifies four.

Vicarious insideness is an identification with a place not visited but experienced vicariously through the stories of others. Reading the diary of a traveller, hearing a place described by a poet or watching a film set in a particular place are all media through which an experience of vicarious insideness may be induced.

Behavioural insideness is a description of a pattern of behaviour which notices where one is. The physical location of the place, the architecture and the building materials employed, the *ambiance* of the place will be noticed. Value judgments will be made about the place based on these observations. McDonald's restaurants may look the same inside and below first floor level the world over but looking up to the higher stories of a building will reveal its age and history. Despite the modifications at street level there is a unique story of building, street and town told and waiting to be heard.

It is possible that a sense of what the place is like will gradually merge into a concern for the place. This is what Relph calls *empathetic insideness*. It is a much richer experience of a place than behavioural insideness for a relation is developed between the symbols and meanings of the place and those which originate from one's own experience. There is here an interplay between the identity of the place, which one must respect, and one's own identity through which one is experiencing the place. Only by being willing to be changed oneself can one fully experience the place as it really is. One might

---

6   E Relph, *Place and Placelessness* (London: Pion, 1976).
7   *Ibid*, p 1.
8   *Ibid*, p 49.

question whether it is ever possible to 'experience the place as it really is'; nevertheless, Relph argues that in certain sorts of relations place can function as an agent changing the identity of a human being.

The most complete sense of insideness is *existential insideness*. This is the sense of belonging to a place: this place and no other is where I belong. One is existentially inside the place where one is subconsciously aware of a wide range of meanings attached to the place and places within it. It is the place where one is accepted as belonging. To be existentially inside a place is to be in a unique relation with a place but also in a unique relation with the people of that place.

To be *existentially outside* a place is both the most complete form of outsideness and the most universal because all human beings have to learn from a very early age to be existentially outside most places. To be outside is to sense, self-consciously, an alienation from the symbols and rituals of a place and its community. There is a sense of not belonging and of being a stranger. This may lead to feelings of rootlessness and homelessness and of insecurity. Moving from one place to another will always lead one to feel existentially outside the new place even if one is determined to 'fit in' and even if one is anxious to develop a sense of empathetic insideness as quickly as possible. In his analysis of life in rural areas Russell shows that these feelings can be very powerful and shape the experience of being in a place:

> '...among some of the unhappiest newcomers [to rural communities] are those young wives whose husbands take the one car to the station or to work; the young wife is left with young children, 'trapped' in a house on a new development on the edge of the village, aware that there is a community life to which she does not relate.'[9]

This is a classic description of the experience of existential outsideness. Such an experience is more acute where fewer people feel it.

Relph identifies two other types of outsideness. Both involve the development of an attitude towards the place which imagines that it is not there or that it is entirely irrelevant to one's existence. *Objective outsideness* is a conscious decision to distance oneself from the reality of the place and to treat it only as a functional object present in the world for certain ends. Modern thought has usually treated places in this way. The recent trend to involve communities in decision making may arise out of the realization that places are more than locations within which powerful feelings are experienced and lives shaped; they are part of the forces which act upon human beings. Modern out-of-town shopping centres would like to pretend that

---

9   A Russell. *A Country Parish* (London: SPCK. 1986) p 173.

they are town centres and would like shoppers to treat them in a 'behaviourally inside' manner—to imagine that we really are where the decor of the mall wants us to think we are. It might be more honest to treat places such as the 'Mediterranean Village' in the Metro Centre in Gateshead as a theme park. It should be used in an objectively outside way for fun. There would be a collusion between owners and users and this would bring meaning to the kitsch.

Finally, *incidental outsideness* is an unconscious experience of an absence of a place. Although McDonald's do not bother to alter the building above shop level they ensure that inside the restaurant it is difficult to tell whether one is in Bangkok or Basildon. Experiences of outsideness are unsettling, they are frequently commented upon, and they are increasingly common.

The human experience of a place is rather more complex than the simple question 'do I feel that this place is "my place"?' The experience of the continuum of insideness/outsideness is universal. Everybody will be able to locate themselves in a number of different points on the continuum in relation to different places and we will be able to remember feeling inside or outside particular places. Places are enormously complex both in their geographical variety and also in the emotions we develop in our relationships with places. The scale at which these emotions can be generated varies considerably. At one end of the scale one may feel 'at home' at home. But familiarity with my street, journey to work, home town or region can also generate feelings of insideness which result in positive experiences for the individual.

Mental Maps: Simplified Places

The complexity of the world which we inhabit is too much for us to take in. Matthew, the central character in *City of the Mind*, saw the complexity of the geography of London reduced to the simple functionality of the Streetfinder atlas or to the practical beauty of the Underground Map. Contours, real road widths, trees, the atmosphere of places are all removed by the need to convey some information simply. If fifty people who worked together all drew a map of their town each map would be different. But the difference would have more to do with the perception of the place by each person and less to do with their cartographic competence—though that would matter too!

In *Anthropology in Theological Perspective* Pannenberg argues that the uniqueness of human beings lies in our ability to step outside ourselves and look at ourselves from the perspective of someone else. This external view leads us to ask questions about the possibility of God, it gives us insight and imagination and it also enables us to make a simplified construct of the world around. All other animals do this but they do so instinctively. Human beings are unique because we know that we simplify the world in order to make greater sense of it.

Places are complexes of interactions between people, the artificial creations of human beings and natural landscapes. Human beings choose to simplify their world by making mental images of places which are more simple than the partially perceived reality around them. It is this partial perception and a subconscious process of simplification which make up the 'imaginative construct' of the world. Human beings acknowledge the existence of only a part of the complex which constitutes a place. This simplifies the world by ignoring those parts of it which are considered unimportant or undesirable. The construction of imaginary pictures of places is necessary because it is impossible to have a complete knowledge of a place, and because it is necessary to understand a place in such a way that one will be able to function effectively within it.[10]

The knowledge an individual possesses of 'their place' will be based on those parts of the place which have special meaning and which they frequent regularly. Consequently, the route to work, to school, to the shops or to the station will form part of the simplified 'mental map' of the place. What is familiar is important and important places feature on the map. Areas not needed by the individual will not feature on the map in such detail.

Places on the mental map also shape the individual, sometimes through social meanings. In many older cities, towns and villages the largest building, at least until the nineteenth century, was a cathedral or a church. The building functioned as a physical form of the presence of God and, often, the wealthy benefactor too. Since the nineteenth century townscapes have been dominated by factories and financial institutions. Technological advancement and economic forces made such buildings possible and also reflected changes in the way that society operated and in the dominant values of the society. There is a circularity in the relationship between the physical form of a place and the dominant social and cultural values held by the people who live in it. As values change and influence building types and styles so new buildings reinforce those values which led to their creation. This mirrors the circularity in the relationship between social structures and cultural forms and between the individual and the corporate in society and culture.

'I Know My Place': Social Placing

Bedford Square in central London, one of many similarly named, is named after the Duke of Bedford on whose land the development was built. Lively gives Matthew the understanding that economic and social power dictates the shape of places; it affects the relationship that each individual has with a

---

[10] See W Pannenberg, *Anthropology in Theological Perspective* (Edinburgh: T & T Clark, 1985) pp 62ff.

WHAT IS PLACE?

place.

Language takes up the theme, and religion, battles and conquests, kings and queens and potentates, that reach back a thousand years or ten, provide a dictionary of reference for those who will listen.

All places, but especially human places, are characterized not only by a physical structure but also by a social structure. Human beings 'know their place' within the community in which they live. They know that the way they behave, the vocabulary they use, the place where they live and a wide variety of other variables reveal where they are located within the social hierarchy of the place.

When we belong to a town or city we understand very clearly which places are 'good' places and which are 'bad' even though the outsider may fail to notice the nuances of the address which launches a thousand prejudices. Human beings organize themselves into a pecking order just as routinely as hens or cows. It may be a more sophisticated order because it is dependent upon a number of variable factors such as class, education, employment, temperament and relative wealth, but it is no less tangible. Location on the pecking order is established at birth but can be varied through life.

Location in space is also dependent, to a significant degree, on the pecking order, and movement through the social hierarchy is constrained by the combination of pecking order and place. House prices are partly dependent upon location. Social organization is reflected in place through economics as well as culture and custom, and these factors in turn limit the ability of the individual to negotiate social and therefore spatial movement.

A place is the locus of social formation, organization and stratification. In any place human society is organized and the rules and patterns of this organization are learnt by young people as they develop into adults. The variations between individuals and groups of people are reflected in a spatial pattern which both reflects and strengthens the social structure of the place. Places are therefore integral to social structure. Institutions regulate human behaviour, mediate social structure and influence the physical form of the place. In turn they too are modified by human behaviour, social structure and the constraints or opportunities afforded by the physical form of the place. It is a matter of fact that almost everybody will feel that they belong more in one sort of place than another—more in a terraced street in a city than in a suburb of inter-war semi-detached houses or more in a flat in a converted warehouse in a riverside redevelopment area than in an out-of-town council estate.

The relation between place and society usually occurs in symbolic forms. The buildings, layout and organization of the place, its physical form, contain cultural statements about the nature of the society which built them.

The existential insider will read these symbolic statements correctly and will consequently 'know her place.' The outsider will not always understand the language being used. So places both result from and help form the social organization of human beings. The social structure which human beings create generates the physical structure which reflects itself and which also goes on to influence and even change it.

Place in Action

When I am in a place I will feel 'at home' or I will feel 'out of place.' This may be because the place does not reflect my place in the social hierarchy, or the subculture is different or I am socially 'out of place.' There is a interrelation between these three experiences of place which renders the distinction between them a device for analysis and description. The human experience of place is a seamless single experience. Whatever the starting point—existential experience, the construction of a simplified place or the experience of social placing—it becomes very difficult to isolate one aspect as the originator of the experience of belonging to or being out of place.

Imagine living on the edge of a modern owner-occupied estate. It is one of the estates people want to live on. An important main road runs along the edge of your estate. It carries traffic from and to all parts of the city and beyond. You live on the edge near the road. On the opposite side of the estate, a 15 minute walk away, there is a small supermarket and a parade of shops, a school, a good pub and a thriving church. It is difficult to drive to these—you need to use roads on the boundary of the estate. The church is in another parish because the stream which forms the boundary is the centrepiece of a well kept park in the middle of the estate. You drive to work some distance away from the estate across the city. If you have children the school has an out-of-hours club for child care. Across the main road from the estate is another estate. It is a poor, though not notorious, council estate in which few houses have been bought. Five minutes away from your house there is another supermarket and parade of shops, though with fewer shops in it, another school, another pub and another (struggling) church.

The purpose of this exercise is not to rehearse a variety of class/cultural prejudices alluded to above but to raise questions about the complex functioning of place. We shall return to the scenario later when thinking about what 'local' means. Consider these questions: Why did you move to your house on the estate? Which parts of both estates are on your mental map? In which estate will you feel 'at home'? Which school would you want your children to go to and why? Which is the nearest pub, in which would you feel most comfortable and why and which pub is your 'local'? Which church would you choose to belong to and why? Do you shop on either estate?

3
Place and Relationships

I make no apology that theology has not yet made a significant appearance! Bible stories might have been used to illustrate the ways in which place operates but this device would have not have served the primary object, understanding place, as effectively as using examples from modern British life. In this more complex section I will offer a summary of how place operates and as we move from geography and anthropology to theology I will describe the relationship between God, place and human beings.

Human beings exist in a place and are part of a complex web of relationships between other human beings who also live in the place and between themselves and the place and its location within a wider locality. This world of relationships is highly complex, for each individual stands in a unique location within the web of relations and views that part of the web which can be seen from her unique perspective. It is not possible to see the whole place in all its complexity and so, in order to function in such a complicated social and physical environment, details are simplified and a less complicated map of the web is constructed, subconsciously, in the mind of the individual. The individual then relates to the place through the simplified map which has been acquired. The map is subject to constant revision and modification. And the perspective of the individual is constrained not only by the community of which she is a part but also by the place of which the community is a part. There is a constant feedback between all the forces which impinge upon each other. In relationships it was always thus.

It is almost impossible to understand the complexity of the relationships which constitute an individual, a community or a place. There are too many, they are too fluid and, in many cases, they are hidden from consciousness. The sense of identity of the self, be it an individual, a culture or a place, sits like a spider at the centre of a huge web. A wide variety of relations and interrelations exist between meeting points on the strand of the web. Each contributes to the whole of the web but it is only at the meeting point, where the spider sits waiting for movement, that the strands, their meeting points, the web itself can be said to have any coherent meaning.

This picture illustrates the sense of identity of a single being but each individual is also a part of another person's web of relations. Similarly, a place is part of my web and I am part of place. The confusion is inevitable. We are used to thinking of identities as discrete, as individuals. But there is an overlap between the identities of human beings; it is what makes us share other people's pain or feel loss when someone dies or we leave a familiar place. And there is clearly overlap between places. It is, quite often, impossible to be sure where one place ends and another begins. There is confusion over scale, function and social geography.

To be placed is to be part of a very wide and complex network of relations which are dynamic by nature. This network is of such complexity and fluidity, however, that it is impossible to understand precisely all the relations in which a person or thing is involved at any one time and place. To be placed, therefore, is to be subject to a variety of forces which are not only beyond the control of the subject but are also, on occasion, beyond the consciousness of the subject, and which must remain so because of their complexity. Conversely, all things function not only as the object of unknown influences but also as their subject, changing them in one way or another.

Where is God?

Hitherto we have only been summarizing what might be described as an anthropology of place. The discussion raises two questions. First, what is the relation between God and the created order and second, what does the Christian understanding of the Trinity say about human relations with God and within creation?

I have argued that objects, animate and inanimate alike, relate to one another and that these objects can be said to be located in these relations. Much modern thought has roots in a Protestant tradition which has risked deism and does not find it easy to share such an understanding. The issue of place reveals the tension between this tradition and newer models of interdependence. The understanding of relations which has been described can be applied to relations not only between human beings and the physical world but also to relations with God who is present in creation as well as being distinct and separate from it.

Places are where human beings meet with one another, with the physical world and also, potentially, with God. They are the context within which relations occur as well as being part of the complex web of relations themselves. In traditional Protestant doctrines of creation God is acknowledged as the creator of the universe who, having completed the act of creation, only then deals directly with his people.[11] Such involvement as there is in the world, which is often perceived as hostile, is frequently the 'supernatu-

---

11 See for example, E Brunner, *Dogmatics Vol. II: The Christian Doctrine of Creation and Redemption* (Lutterworth: Lutterworth Press, 1952) where it is clear that, while Protestant theology has not been deistic, speaking of God working in and through creation is difficult. See also Luther in his commentary on Romans, *Library of Christian Classics Vol XV: Luther on Romans*, W Pauck (ed) (London: SCM, 1961) pp 238-9 and, more starkly, Calvin, for whom the function of creation is to *point* man to God. Its beauty informs humanity of God; it does not embody the Spirit of God. See J Calvin, *Institutes of the Christian Religion*, trans H Beveridge (London: J Clarke, 1962) I xiv 21 and 22, pp 156, 157.

ral' act of God revealing himself to his people in history. It is this theology of creation which informs a hostility to the possibility that God relates to his people in sacramental presence while thought and memory are acceptable media for the presence of God.

The incarnation is of universal significance because God became a particular human being at a particular time and in a particular place. All human beings share the uniqueness of being in one place at one time. It has been traditional to maintain that God is present in *universal* place if he is present in place at all. He is in all places, therefore he must be here. However, by analogy with the incarnation, it is only by being present in a particular place that God can be said to be present in all places. The notion of the *Shekinah* describes the indwelling of God in a particular place. It expresses the truth that God is present in creation, and therefore in places, and in this way dwells amongst people. It is only because God dwells in one particular place that it is possible to say that he also dwells in all other places. 'The God who in the Spirit dwells in his creation is present to every one of his creatures...'[12]

It is because God is the creator of all things that he is present in all things and that, therefore, all things are in relation to God. In summarizing his intention in writing *God in Creation* Moltmann writes that 'the triune God not only stands over against his creation but also at the same time enters into it through his eternal spirit, permeates all things and through his indwelling brings about the community of creation.'[13] McFadyen argues that God is present in the transformed relations between human beings. This presence is unconditional and is guaranteed by the creative activity of God.[14] God is present in a particular place and therefore in all places by the indwelling of his Spirit. So to be in relationship with a place, however construed, is to be in relation with God.

God is present in creation, in this place, now, in such a way that he participates in the web of relations which I am. He is present by virtue of my faith but also by being present in the place where I am and which forms, in part at least, who I am. But he is also in this place in a creative and freeing manner in which trust is given and which is redemption:

'When we think of this in trinitarian terms, it suggests a God whose perfection is perfected (or expanded) in the original and ongoing act of conferring the freedom of otherness on human beings and is fulfilled in so far as it is ongoingly responded to by human beings through their conferral of an otherness upon God which has the character of trust. Indeed, there is a gratuitous freeing on both sides, based on dedication and

---

12 See J Moltmann, *God in Creation* (London: SCM, 1985) pp 13-16.
13 J Moltmann, *History and the Triune God* (London: SCM, 1991) p 181.
14 See A McFadyen, *The Call To Personhood* (Cambridge: CUP, 1990).

trust...through which the freeing is never arbitrary. The same is the basis for the community of human beings.'[15]

The completion of human beings can only take place in the response to God's love by offering love in return. However,

> 'The way in which all this happens is not only, or even primarily, with singular human beings. For God is concerned with the common humanity of human beings; and the trinitarian agency which is implicit in believing is also operative in the constitution of a "new communion of persons in society and the wider creation."'[16]

Hardy refers to the trinitarian basis of what he calls elsewhere 'created sociality.'[17] The community of the trinity is the driving force behind the establishment and the operation of open, trusting societies just as much as it is behind the act of believing of human beings. And it is the driving force behind the establishment of open, trusting relations with place too.

To be placed is to be part of a very wide and complex network of relations which are dynamic by nature. But it is also to be placed in relation to God as mediated by all the other relations in which one is engaged. By being present in all things God is mediated to an individual through, or rather by being in, all the rich variety of relations which constitute the being of any particular individual. And God is to be found in each of these relations. God stands outside these relations, outside place and outside creation, both judging and saving. A full account of the relationship between creation and salvation, the love of the immanent God in place and the judgment of the transcendent God towards whom we journey, cannot be addressed in this booklet.

The issue of the theological account of place focuses the issue of relationships and being. But it is not possible to account for being, for social organization, or for the manner in which God is present in creation or makes himself known to human beings without also addressing the question of the theol-

---

15 D Hardy. 'A Magnificent Complexity.' in D Ford & D Stamps (eds) *Essentials of Christian Community* (Edinburgh: T & T Clark. 1996) p 318. There is no space to give a full account of implications of relational thinking on our understanding of redemption.

16 D Hardy. *op cit*, p 319. Hardy is responding to Stephen Pickard's chapter 'The Trinitarian Dynamics of Belief in the same book. We cannot describe Hardy's trinitarian thinking here but he states that 'the very act of believing, its formation and sharing, are loci for the dynamic realization of the work of the triune God.' and he refers approvingly to Pickard's suggestion that 'it is of the nature of the triune God to be implicated in the believing of human beings as the church.' 'God is present in the believing such that belief is Spirited along in a manner which honours the God of Jesus Christ.' as Spirited response to the gift of God in Jesus Christ. (p 317).

17 D Hardy. 'Created and Redeemed Sociality' in C Gunton & D Hardy (eds) *On Being the Church*. (Edinburgh: T & T Clark. 1989).

ogy of place. The observation that to be is to be placed in a physical location, in a social hierarchy and in a constructed world view and that God is present in all these relations is fundamental to all theological discussion. And, in addition to this, the manner of God's trinitarian being and his presence in creation informs the nature of created, relational, social being and the possibility of the transformation of relations. In the last section we will see that this trinitarian understanding of place can inform questions of the theology and practice for the church, for ministry and even for mission.

4
Place and Church

In the last chapter we will consider more practical issues which arise out of the theory described above. In asking 'where is the local church?' I will address the issues concerning the nature of the church, the object of its mission and the value of the traditional parish structure of the Church of England. I will ask what implications a complex understanding of locality has for appropriate structures for the staffing and leadership of churches in a changing culture. The context of postmodernism encourages us to seek solutions to problems which we believe preserve important truths of the gospel, which understand the working of our trinitarian God and which respond to the ways in which people in Britain tend to behave but which are not neat or simple to operate. Robert May wrote in 1976 'Not only in research, but in the everyday world of politics and economics, we would all be better off if more people realized that simple systems do not necessarily possess simple dynamic properties.'[18] The same might be true of the practice of the church.

Where is Local?

'Bethany was less than two miles from Jerusalem and many Jews had come to Martha and Mary to comfort them in the loss of their brother' (John 14.18-19). Many Jews were prepared to walk the two miles from Jerusalem to grieve with their friends. These two miles will have seemed further to those who lived in Jerusalem and rarely walked to Bethany than to people from Bethany who regularly walked to Jerusalem, for whom the journey was familiar. Locality is uneven and is not only to do with distance.

---

18 I Stewart. *Does God Play Dice* (London: Penguin. 1989) p 21.

In the exercise above at the end of chapter 2 it is likely that the inhabitants of the house on the new estate would not feel 'at home' on the estate across the main road. That estate would not feature in their mental map. They would go to the pub on 'their' estate fifteen minutes away. This pub, surely, is the local. The point is that the question of locality must be seen in a more sophisticated a way than simply believing that 'closest' means 'most local.'

What constitutes locality has not changed. Locality is to do with familiarity. However, what is near (local) is assumed to be what is familiar because that is how things used to be. It is only in relatively recent historical times that significant numbers of people have journeyed to work or moved away from the place where they were brought up. The mobility implied by the journey to work, or in more recent times to the sports centre, golf club, shopping centre or multi-screen cinema renders places familiar which previously would have been quite unknown to the residents of the place one inhabits. But the places with which I am familiar need not be the places that feel local to my neighbour. These places are now known because they are on my mental map—I know the way to the supermarket; they are frequented by like-minded people—people like me because they can afford to shop here; they are places where I feel at home—the atmosphere creates an environment where I feel I belong.

It is well known that where we live may not be the place where we feel that we belong because in modern society many people (though by no means all) find that they belong in a more disparate way in a number of separate locations which they choose to go to from home. These separate locations are local places, but they are not physically near the home. These separate locations are near in the existential sense of being a place where one feels one belongs; they are near in the sense that they feel closer than somewhere geographically closer because they are on the mental map; and they are near in the social sense because they are filled with like-minded people. It is not that we do not belong at home, but that the street, village town or suburb in which the home is placed is frequently unimportant. So the 'local' pub need not be the nearest because locality is no longer expressed only in geographical distance.

However, the unimportance of the proximate is not neutral. To say 'No' to a neighbour, 'local' school, pub, church or corner shop is a powerful statement. The act of driving past people and services on the way to somewhere else may be subconscious but it is, nevertheless, a positive action which is a rejection of the nearby in favour of the familiar or conducive. It is similar to refusing to say 'hello' or 'good morning' to someone we know when we meet them. An understanding of locality needs to be found which acknowledges the importance of existential belonging, mental map familiarity or social homogeneity but which does not treat the nearby as invisible.

Ways of Being Church

The origins of the modern parish system are complex. The Celtic church, particularly in Ireland, appears to have organized itself following the notion of the 'paruchia' or sphere of influence of senior clergy of diocese or monastery.[19] There was also a significant influence from the more administrative mind-set of the Augustinian Mission. Anglo-Saxon and Anglo-Norman responses to Gregorian reforms and the need to find an effective way to fund church building and the maintenance of ministry encouraged the development of territories attached to churches.[20]

Today, we have two modes of being the church. Most of us think of the church in its parochial mode. Its sphere of influence is a small geographical area. Usually relations across parish boundaries are matters of convenience and courtesy and are not crossed for sharing either mission or ministry. There are 'non-parochial' modes which do not use geography to define their 'sphere of existence': theological colleges, churches for minority or national groups such as the deaf or Lutheran congregations and sector ministry such as chaplaincies or industrial mission.

Some churches do not operate on the 'parish' model, though they usually have parishes. These 'eclectic' churches often describe themselves as 'local' churches but by this they mean a congregation.[21] In practice, it is often a church not of a geographical location but of like-minded people who feel at home in the social and churchmanship environment the church provides. Such 'network' churches serve particular needs and serve them well because, by definition, the members of the church may be facing similar problems. It is likely that eclectic churches will also be more 'successful.' For this reason, and in this sense, they are more comfortable to belong to. These 'niche' churches may cater not just for socially similar people but also for people of similar profession or social situation. Black churches, student churches and the church for the deaf are fulfilling very similar functions.[22] In each case it may be true that the 'niche' church offers more than an 'ordinary' parish church but feelings of having been excluded from parish churches suggests that there may be a denial of the gospel present. These stand in the monastic tradition of modes of being the church. Robert Warren sums up the inherited attitude of the Church of England:

---

19 See R Sheldrake, *op cit*, especially pp 10-18.
20 See R E Rodes Jnr, *Ecclesiastical Administration in Mediaeval England: The Anglo-Saxons to the Reformation* (Notre Dame: University of Notre Dame Press, 1977) especially pp 19-31.
21 It might be added that they may sometimes be guilty of applying a modern, individualist reading to the use of 'congregation' in the 39 Articles.
22 These observations are independently arrived at in *Breaking New Ground: Church Planting in the Church Of England* (London: Church House, 1994) GS1099. This study offers a new perspective on these observations by linking the tripartite pattern of territory, neighbourhood, network (pp 1-4) to an understanding of locality.

'The result of this long process has been that we understand the church as the parish church, working in a defined geographical and social grouping.'[23]

Being the 'Local' Church

For a variety of reasons—some good, some bad and some inevitable—we have constructed a set of rules or imperatives about the parish boundary. There is the law to do with marriage, courtesies to follow about baptisms, payment of fees, where one 'ought' to go to church and so on. But most people do not know where the parish boundary is, and if they did they would not care.[24] Parish boundaries were set in very different demographic and cultural times. What was once a sensible boundary between two parishes along a stream is now a boundary down the middle of a road.

The parish is necessary if we are to preserve the heterogeneity in our church communities which the gospel demands but it must be made to operate in a very untidy, flexible way so that the boundaries between the two modes of being the church are blurred and the validity of both modes is widely accepted.

A local church is a church which an individual feels is his or her local church. And this feeling of localness can be inspired by a sense of belonging or familiarity with the people, the physical location, or the church tradition and theology. It would be possible to say that the parish is an irrelevance, that worshipping in like-minded communities is a fact of human behaviour and cannot be resisted. But this is not an option. Ignoring neighbours, the street and town on the way to somewhere else is not a neutral act. It affects our being and changes who we are. Creating an ecclesial structure in which churches do not discourage the temptation to homogeneity would be a denial of the gospel. 'There is no such thing as Jew and Greek, slave and freeman, male and female; for you are all one person in Christ Jesus' (Gal 3. 28). God and human beings are social by nature and our contemporary denial of this is also a denial of what it is to be human. In the previous section we showed that to be a Christian is to be part of a people. As Warren puts it:

> 'Where the Christians, and indeed much modern psychology, would want to point to another perspective is that we are not only manifestly 'social beings,' but that by our very nature we are 'beings-in-relationship.' This is expressed in the social nature of God as Trinity, and is a major theme of

---

[23] R Warren. *Being Human, Being Church* (London: Marshall Pickering. 1995) p 27. It is not at all clear that 'parish' churches do operate within a defined social grouping. and this is part of the problem.

[24] This is obviously a much bigger problem in towns and cities but it can be just as real in villages especially where new development on the edge of a village crosses ecclesial boundaries which mean little to anybody else.

a range of modern theologians. We are not sealed units but part of a committed community. Independence is a stage on the road to maturity which itself is marked by interdependence.'[25]

In *Practising Community: The Task of the Local Church* Robin Greenwood proposes a radical change in way the church organizes itself. He suggests:

'My own vision for the future that is emerging, in response to all the factors mentioned already, is of local churches that take in very wide swathes of territory, so that inherited ministerial arrangements, already under review, will continually need adjustment. The parish system with its many buildings must now be secondary to the redevelopment of the idea of the local church as a locally negotiated area of collaborative ministry.'[26]

This suggestion (under the heading 'The Whole of the Church in Every Place') is very similar to solutions found in Lincoln Diocese in a context of very small parishes and very few clergy. Ian Stockton, Local Ministry Officer in Lincoln, made similar 'macro-parish' suggestions in an article in *Theology*. The Lincoln solution is to think in terms of the 'pastoral unit' for which an individual stipendiary minister has oversight rather than an ancient parish. This may be as many as twelve 'parishes.' He acknowledges the untidiness of the solution:

'Whilst taking other disciplines such as geography and sociology into careful account we should not be daunted by the difficulty of localness, or dispirited by searching after impossible precision. What is important is that the Church in its planning, provision of worship, pastoral care and mission, goes within the grain of the landscape, social networks and natural belonging as far as it is possible.'[27]

Stockton's solution is particular to Lincoln Diocese and the problem of multi-benefice clergy and tiny parishes is not the major problem in most dioceses, though few do not have to grapple with it at some scale.

Greenwood's suggestion, which involves enlarging the parish boundary (or at least working with new geographical limits to territory 'owned' by a 'local' church), is a pragmatic solution to present problems but it does not

---

25 R Warren. *op cit*. p 45.
26 R Greenwood. *Practising Community: The Task of the Local Church* (London: SPCK. 1996) p 26.
27 I Stockton. p 357. 'What is Local?' in *Theology*. Vol XCV. No. 767. 1992. pp 353-360. Further. important comments about the relation between the church local and the church catholic are also made but there is not the space to deal with the issue in this booklet.

address the real problem. The problem is that locality is no longer a matter of geography. A church congregation ten minutes from home might be more unfamiliar than a lunch-time congregation near work fifty miles away. The 'very wide swathes of territory' which each local church would need to cover cannot remove the problem of the boundary or the 'patchy' nature of complex locality. There are always edges to a territory and blind spots in a mental map.

Parish Boundaries

Stockton and Greenwood are happy to acknowledge that neatness is neither a priority nor a possibility. It seems to me that the existing parish boundaries need to be left roughly as they are. The principle for this is the importance of the parish in reminding churches of the communal and relational nature of the gospel. It is a symbol of its emplacement. It is a pragmatic suggestion because there is no possibility of creating geographically-defined areas which reflect natural human associations. And it is so difficult to change parish boundaries that it hardly seems worth the effort needed for such little reward.

If parish boundaries are to be retained then churches must sit very lightly to them. There are two implications for church life. It should not be difficult for lay people to move from one church to another and back again. And it should be assumed that clergy and lay leaders will exercise ministry in parishes other than their own. The goal at the end of a generation-long cultural change in the church is that leaders will practice collaborative ministry as the natural way to lead churches and lay people will ask how their gifts can be best used in the locality or which church would best serve the next stage in their spiritual journey. Lay people will want to identify with particular congregations for all the reasons described above and, if possible, it may be that clergy will be identified with particular parishes too. But it need not be inevitable that the parish boundary represents a barrier to shared ministry and broadened experience.

Which parishes will work with each other must be a locally agreed arrangement. It is not easy to require people to work together and forcing parishes who are adjacent to go beyond cooperation and move to collaboration will not work. But at the same time clergy, and to a lesser extent lay leaders, need to recognize that demands for theological purity, liturgical correctness or trendy issue alertness prevent the church from serving the community and thus prevent it from being itself. The neighbouring parish with a very different theology or church tradition may offer members of 'my' church just what they need either permanently or, more likely, in the short term. At present the richness of the variety of the Church of England is denied to many ordinary church members.

It may be that the demands of bureaucracy for neatness and order and the stubbornness of church leaders who refuse to work with other church leaders for a variety of reasons or who are unwilling to give up control will lead dioceses to take the Greenwood approach.[28] But it would be much better if clergy pride, demands for spurious doctrinal or sacramental purity, or anxieties and insecurities were not allowed to prevent a genuine local pattern of collaboration to emerge. This is no easy, simple or clear cut matter but post-modern times may demand solutions to problems which acknowledge the absence of single neat answers to questions of relationships and working together.[29]

The implication of clergy collaborating is that we are unlikely to need an omnicompetent individual who delivers ministry to a passive congregation. Stipendiary clergy *may* find themselves leading churches but would also be able to develop their skills and interests and offer these to a wider group of congregations. This might result in most work being done by clergy (or laity) to a higher standard and may yield greater job satisfaction amongst clergy who are widely believed to be suffering from low morale. At the very least it may cut the link between the success or well being of 'my parish' and my feeling of self worth. If ministry in each church is shared amongst clergy and skilled, trained laity then the success or failure of a church is the result of team work not individual effort. Of course, the stress of working in a team may replace the stress of working 'alone'…!

The trust and familiarity built amongst clergy and lay leaders in this way should mean that it will be easier for lay people to belong to a church which is not their parish church. And it will also be easier for them to move from one church to another. It must be right for a charismatic evangelical to attend a church which reflects their tradition even if it is not their parish church. But if the leadership of all the churches in an area are collaborating then it is possible that that individual might be encouraged to attend an Anglo-Catholic church for a while because the style of worship will suit an aspect of the person's spirituality which the charismatic cannot (and does not want to) serve. They might be encouraged to belong to the church because it has become clear that as they have grown and developed the Catholic spirituality of the other church is what is appropriate for them for the foreseeable future. Or they might be encouraged to move churches because they have a particular skill which the other church needs at the moment. There is no

---

28 It is not the practice of parishes being linked together that is questioned but the theory behind the links. The dynamics behind church membership are more complex than mere atlas geography because geography is about more than maps.

29 Space limits the possibility of describing the role of diocese which needs to be representative (of catholicity) and responsive (to parochial schemes)—*Breaking New Ground* p 3. Public prayer for the bishop as well as deanery, network or link churches fosters a sense of unity and self-identity.

PLACE: CHURCH AND MISSION

reason why this movement should not happen in any direction. And this collaboration need not be restricted to churches of one denomination.

The responsibility of eclectic, network churches in this system is to use their character and scale to provide a service for other churches. Network evangelism, major events, liturgical specialisms and excellence, use of the arts in worship and a regional or national profile are often possible in an eclectic church at a scale beyond the resources of other churches. But eclectic churches also need to produce lay people who are able to join other churches having been introduced or refreshed by their life. They need also to be able to accept people who will be looking for a short term period of refreshment or to broaden their spirituality. Eclectic churches are not for hiding in, at least not for too long.

This argument can also be extended beyond different modes of parish and eclectic churches who recognize that their task is common to other non-geographical modes of being church. At present there appears to be very little contact between sector ministers and their parochial colleagues even though they both have care of the same people. A proper understanding of locality can lead to the establishment of trust and collaboration between very different modes of being the church. For example, it is often said that parish churches find it difficult to relate faith and work but the church, through industrial mission, has been in the work place for some time.[30]

In this brief analysis we have shown how place operates, outlined a theological understanding of the presence of God in place and sketched some suggestions for the practice of the church. Space has prevented deeper consideration in each of these areas. It has not been possible to offer a discussion of the role of the diocese or of mission organizations and churches overseas. The aim has been to encourage a more sophisticated understanding of place, locality and collaboration in ministry and mission amongst the people of God.

---

30 'The church' here means the church in its visible form through the clergy. The church, the people of God in a place, has always been in the workplace.